I Feel,
Therefore I Am

John James Cooper

Copyright © 2020 by John James Cooper

All rights reserved. No part of this publication may be reproduced, stored in a retrieval system, or transmitted in any form or by any means, electronic, mechanical, photocopying, recording or otherwise, without the prior written permission of the copyright holders.

The author may be contacted at jjcooper39@hotmail.com

EP&J2 PUBLISHING
Crawford, Tennessee

ISBN 978-1-7355600-0-7

Library of Congress Control Number 2020915804

This book is dedicated to
Esther Pauline Cooper,
who helped me find my way.

Contents

Acknowledgments 7

Introduction 9

Eviction 13

Loneliness 17

Locked in Box 75 23

Enchanted 25

Man's Remains 26

Innocence Lost 29

Satan's Circle 30

The Plague 31

The Darkness 32

Resolution 33

The Journey 34

Achievement's Folly 35

Second Chance 36

The Garden 37

Endless 38

Always 40

Possession	41
God's Postcard	45
Why He Made Me Wait	46
The Final Lullaby	47
Epitaph	48

Acknowledgments

When I completed the manuscript for this book, I was feeling pretty good with myself. I then turned to the task of transforming these pages into a *published* book. That is when reality slapped me square in the face. Have you ever been lost in the woods, looking in all directions, but have no idea of which way to go? That was me. But, thank God, I am the most fortunate of men. I have a wife who is not only beautiful but also possesses a number of valuable skills. She has been kind enough to exercise those skills so that my writing finally made it to publication. I am so grateful that she was willing to use her notable social, organizational, and administrative skills to see this project through to fruition.

We were so lucky to find an exceptional and meticulous editor in Judi Heidel at Perfectly Clear Editing Services. She was more than patient, correcting the endless errors in my grammar and punctuation. What is most amazing is that she made all these corrections without sacrificing my voice and the intent of the pieces in this book. Thank you, Judi.

With Judi's help, we found Julie Klein at JKlein-Editor. She agreed to format the manuscript and prepare it for the chosen publication platform. She did an excellent job ensuring that the book's contents met the necessary publication requirements as well as attaining the professional look we were hoping for. Thank you, Julie, for all your help.

In our search for a cover designer, Julie referred us to Mi Ae Lipe at What Now Design. In a bit of a twist, Mi Ae was not able to fit us into her schedule for the cover design, but she has turned out to be our professional advisor, our guide if you will. She has been such a tremendous help to us as we navigated our way to the completion of this project. Mi Ae's knowledge base related to all aspects of publishing is vast. Thank you, Mi Ae, for all your advice, direction, and information sharing. It has made all the difference.

For help with our cover design, Mi Ae referred us to Robert Lanphear at Lanphear Design. Robert was able to create a design that was not only eye-catching but also expressed the true essence of the book's contents. Great work, Robert. Thank you so much.

As you can see, referrals allowed my wife and me to access a network of highly efficient professionals, all of whom exceeded our expectations. We are grateful to them all.

If anyone cares to reach me, my email address is jjcooper39@hotmail.com.

Introduction

You can write a memoir by focusing on the physical details of what happened along your journey. Another approach is to focus on the emotional content of your life's events. It is, after all, the specific emotions of particular events that make up our memories and, in turn, tell the story of our lives. Each of us possesses a unique set of sensibilities, which function as the primary factors in an unconscious process that is constantly selecting what is saved in permanent memory and what is discarded in the bottomless void of the forgotten past. Emotions paint the circumstance of our everyday existence, and they determine the mood, the tone, the intensity, and the relevance of the various happenings that make up our personal pilgrimage from birth to death. Fortunately, we have some flexibility with regard to how our memories are colored. Most of us have a tendency to lighten up our darkest moments, just a bit, and to brighten up our happiest moments to a sunshine yellow. This balances out the tapestry and allows us to live more comfortably with ourselves. Some might argue that this flexibility leads to a distortion of the emotions that one actually experienced during a particular event. I believe that an individual's feelings are the most personal and private of all possessions. Who's to say, other than you, what color of paint to use?

Eviction

In Norfolk, Virginia, on a September evening, I was forcefully expelled from the safe and controlled environment of my mother's womb. I protested this eviction by crying out and squirming about in a useless effort to find my way back in. Apparently, my lease had expired, and my eviction was permanent. I was now a prisoner of this new world. It was a horrifying place. Upon my arrival, I fell into the sticky latex-covered extremities of some faceless creatures, whose bodies were enshrouded in caps and gowns. Yes, my vision was extremely poor, but still I could make out those ghostly figures moving about in the room making unintelligible sounds. My resistance to being forced into this new world did not subside due to the exhaustion of my physical energy but rather was due to being overwhelmed by stimuli. Numerous unfamiliar smells rampaged through my newly activated olfactory nerves. Ultrasensitive tactile nerve endings, which were accustomed to an ultraprotective environment, were now fully exposed to the constant irritations of those eerie figures touching, turning, and generally manhandling me. The air moved about me, irritating my skin, whenever one of the figures darted past, or I was passed around, or a door opened or closed, or even when a sheet or blanket was simply lifted then dropped. Temperatures seemed to go up then down, like a thermostatic rollercoaster, leaving me overheated one moment, then chilled to the bone at the next. Endless shapes and shadows passed through my undeveloped visual field, but instead of appearing as individual things, they all seemed to be part of a whole, like a motion picture film running rapidly through the length and breadth of this new world. Light was the worst, bright and glaring. There was no relief from it, ever—overhead lights, bedside lights, night lights, clock lights, equipment lights, pen lights, light coming in from an open door or from a crack under the door, streetlights, and starlight creeping in from the night. All of this in stark contrast to the soothing and complete darkness of my previous home. Sounds were just plain shocking, especially with my limited vision, which made it impossible to connect sounds with their causes. Yes, I was a bit prepared for sounds. I had heard them for some time through the thin walls of my old residence, but that was like hearing them from a distance, muffled and soft to the ear. In this world, sounds were distinct, and they were all very loud. It could best be described as if the world was yelling at you and just would not stop, no matter how much you wished it would. It left me in a constant state of being startled or waiting to be startled. If I could have formed thoughts to ask a question, it would have gone something like this: I was a creation of God who was living in a creation of God; I was without sin. What could I possibly have done to deserve being ejected from the body of heaven, my mother's womb, the closest thing to paradise? I had woken to a world that was a constant barrage of painful and anxiety-producing irritations, which you know, even before you have words to say it, will never end. If I could have found a single word to describe it, it would have been "hell."

I was further terrorized by being poked, prodded, stabbed, washed (in a rather rough fashion), and wrapped with my arms secured like a felon who might shank someone if given the opportunity. Finally, I was tossed into a plastic, see-through box and carted off. I eventually arrived at my destination and was parked at a bedside. When my escort left, there were only two entities present in the immediate space. It was quieter here. Surprisingly, the voices of the two present were familiar, but one stole my entire attention. As a twenty-week-old fetus, her voice was one of the first sounds I had ever heard. It was so ingrained in me that I would always be able to recognize it, even in a crowd of thousands. I was picked up and laid against the one who had that irresistible voice. I knew her smell immediately—just as well, if not better, than I knew her voice. I had lived with her body being my body for so long that her smell could not be mistaken. And when my face was laid against her chest, my skin was her skin, as it had always been. I wanted desperately for us to merge back into one person. But lying there was as close as I could ever possibly get to being back in that perfect and peaceful world that was now far away, deep inside my mother's being. I could not get there, but snuggled up against her body, I could hear my old place of residence echoing through her—the sloshing about of internal organs, especially the intestines twisting and gurgling, the methodical digestion process going on in her stomach, the constriction and relaxation of her major blood vessels in sync with her heart. Yes, her heart, that thing that made the magical music, music that entertained me, comforted me, and lulled me to sleep when I used to float in my warm bed of amniotic fluids. No, I could never get back home. Everything from here on out was a moving away from perfection.

Loneliness

(My Twin and My Friend)

In the womb is where it all began, when Loneliness became my closest friend, born when I was born, like an invisible twin.

In the crib he lay with me, unseen by loving eyes, the answer to their question of why I seldom cried.

He kept me company in corners of rooms while other clumsy infants performed cheap, little tricks to assure that they were cuddled, diapered, and fed.

Hidden within the folds of Mother's flowing dress, we peeked out, while tyrannical toddlers screamed out their demands to maternal bond servants who were paying penance for their sins by conceiving a life that now stole their lives from them.

In miniature desks, sitting far in the back, we watched other friendships develop then crash — flimsy affairs due to desperate despair when deserted by mothers at the schoolmaster's door for a brain-washing session of twelve years or more.

Off to the side, in playgrounds and parks, we observed pubescent robots, programmed for their parts, in amazing displays of refined social arts.

From niches in high school hallways, we endured the stampedes of migrating masses of hormonal teens. They settled and gathered in hierarchical packs, their rank predetermined by their weakness or strength; accepting their places in the social regime, then living out lives of unfulfilled dreams.

In adulthood we stumbled from here and to there, a constantly restless and transient pair. Futile attempts to fit in led to awkward encounters that had tragic ends. We were condemned to mingle with misfits who lived on the fringe, at a masquerade party that had no end. We avoided our pain by fulfilling our whims as predators of neurotic women who possessed a masochistic need for cold, sadistic lovers, men who could never be pleased. As malicious marauders without conscience or guilt, we took from others and gave to ourselves. Intoxicated with rage, we forged ahead, ignoring road signs that warned of "Danger Ahead."

In silent reflection, Loneliness sat beside me in cell blocks reserved for human debris. But still not content, we went straight down to hell, to the bowels of the prison in an isolation cell. There I laughed, I cried, and I talked to myself until my mental stability lost hold of itself. Uninvited visions crept through the walls, whispering the blessings of ending it all. But at last my good friend, who was quite fed up, called me a bitch and yelled, "Shut the fuck up!"

Released to society on our final reprieve, we tried for normality, that hypnotic state called the American dream—more like a nightmare of obligations and routines that relied on a constant monetary stream. We were paroled to a sentence of indentured servitude to assure that the dreams of others came true—from spouses lost in marital bliss with dreams of Mercedes floating in their heads, to mortgage holders who gleamed with delight that interest times four was their God-given right, to parsons demanding their 10 percent while abusing their sacred scripts in order to assure you of their righteous intent.

We broke our parole and escaped to a hut on an isolated lot far away on a hidden mountaintop. There we were safe from the dream of "getting ahead," with its deadlines, schedules, and working weekends; safe from the demands of trying to fit in with the conventional thinking of conditional friends; safe from a lover's love of monetary means and her affairs with credit limits to meet limitless needs; safe from the benevolence of the Church and the State, who bribe you with trinkets and threaten your soul, offering you the freedom to do what you're told.

Loneliness and I were pondering the depths of our discontented soul when Death arrived banging on the door. He was an ill-tempered sort who invited himself in, then stood in every shadow with his stark yellow eyes, mumbling and grumbling about quotas he must make and how rude I was for making him wait. Death drew close and, as hard as I tried, I was powerless to avoid the stare of his unblinking eyes. He whispered in a deep, rumbling voice, "Loneliness is real but not like you think. It is not a person, your twin, or your friend. That is just something you made up in your head. At best, he's a reflection of your own sordid soul. It's been only you, **only you,** all along."

Death enjoyed causing me pain, and so he took his time to further explain. "Loneliness is such a fearful thing that most people spend their lives trying to avoid it. But you embraced loneliness when you needed a friend; when you were alone and afraid in the crib; when others more skilled stole attention from you; when you turned out odd and could not fit in, set adrift to live out on the fringe; when faced with the horrors of an isolation cell; when you needed an excuse for not killing yourself; when others abused you till nothing remained, all for the sake of their own personal gain. Yes, loneliness is real but not like you think. That delusion helped you deal with the pain of being estranged from a world full of people who saw you as strange. Now enough of this talk. I must be on my way. I have a schedule to keep, and you're slowing my pace."

Just at that moment, Loneliness appeared, assuring me that there was nothing to fear, "Don't let this trash talker get in your head, we started together and together we'll end." Death seemed astonished as he stared at my twin, but Loneliness stared right back, not giving an inch. "You crusty corpse counter, what's your big rush? Do you think someone will miss you if you're late showing up? Now you've had your fun tormenting my friend. Step back I say—don't make me tell you again." Taking my hand, Loneliness gave it a squeeze and said, "This life was not kind. It's been a rough trip. Let's wrap up this party and move on to the next. Now let me assure you, where we're going, we've been; we're only returning to where we began. Before we were born, we were but a bit of light in a great, dark abyss where no pretense exists, no thoughts or worries of how to fit in, no one to please or appease, no fear of rejection, and no bowing nor bending of knee. It is an endless expanse sprinkled with lights like fireflies in the darkness of a warm summer's night."

With this I was prepared to meet our fate, and together we made our final escape: a calming silence, a loss of sight, an absence of breath, a blissful relaxation that made our body feel light, a quiet implosion that shattered our soul and propelled our remains to the heart of creation, where Loneliness and I wait on regeneration.

Locked in Box 75

The value of solitude grew with time as my need for others slowly declined.

My heart hardened and my emotions ceased, mercifully stifling the hope of reprieve.

Alone in the darkness of my cubical space, I kept myself company, became my best friend, and taught myself to never rely on others again.

I was naked and crouched in the corner when the light blinded me. But when I finally could look at them, they knew it wasn't me.

In my eyes they saw no respect for others nor any self-esteem, no kindness nor mercy—just a vicious, heartless beast.

I had extracted that gnawing gregarious need, which had become a cognitive malignancy— relentlessly eating away at me.

It required considerable effort to remove that piece of humanity, as it was rooted deep inside of me. And though it caused excruciating pain, I dug deeper to ensure that none remained: no seed of need for others could be left to germinate.

They did not see the tumor; I had flushed it down a drain. But still they knew that something was missing and that, somehow, I had changed.

They saw that I had used my blood to decorate the walls by finger-painting a landscape of some internal hell that they could not imagine, but that I knew all too well

They smelled the urine and feces that covered most of me—a baptism of sorts to say goodbye to the past and to set my new self free.

They closed the metal door behind them as they back stepped their way out. They knew there would be hell to pay when they tried to get me out.

Enchanted

A rosebud blossomed, the brightest of them all.

It stood upon a hard, strong stem that would not let it fall.

Its foliage gave it grace and class, but its thorns warned of their given task.

Finally a gardener came one day, and with skill he stole the rose away.

The gardener and the rose were enchanted, and the beauty of the rose lasted and lasted.

The rose finally faded but only on cue, for when the gardener died, the rose died too.

Man's Remains

The truth of True Love dropped on him like a great weight. It crushed his knees and splintered his tibiae, forcing him into a humbled position. There, kneeling, he realized that an emotional artery had been severed and that his will to live was flowing out, forming a great multi-colored pool that surrounded him.

He fell back into a sitting position of sorts, intentionally leaving his vital organs exposed. It was there, in his empty castle, on the waxed hardwood floor, that Reality's sword disemboweled him, leaving but a little spark of life that he prayed would soon be extinguished.

His hands, which once held hope in an iron grip, were ripped off at the wrists and discarded by the back screen door. A half-starved alley cat peeked in and became excited by the possibility of an easy meal. It paced about, sniffing and scratching, trying to find a way in.

The man felt a tugging sensation under his left rib cage, which finally succeeded in tearing out the pain that was in his chest. In a semiconscious state, he spent the last few moments of that life watching his eviscerated heart being slammed against the unpainted walls. The few remaining emotions, hidden deep within the atria and ventricles, were forced out, splattering against the bare sheetrock, making a mess that contained a message like a Jackson Pollock painting. What remained of that organ, that mangled, worn-out heart, bounced feebly about the room like an old well-used rubber chew toy, finally disappearing through the open basement door, never to be seen again.

His love-struck eyes, once full of lust for the object of their desire, went dim—then blank. He was past knowing or caring when those eyes were plucked out. Those orbs, which had seen beautiful visions, now lay in an empty corner of the room—food for a swarm of ants.

Yes, there were cries of pain and many pleas for mercy. They echoed off the walls, but they all went unheard, drowned out by the loud parade of life, which constantly marched on outside the living room window.

His passing went unnoticed. In time his remains decomposed, until little was left except for a thin exoskeleton, which only vaguely resembled what the man had been.

A door flew open, a wind blew through, and that dry, fragile shell of man's remains shattered, then scattered, throughout the room.

Eventually a visitor came to the vacant castle looking for the man who had once resided there, but he found only sunlight shining through undraped windows and remnant dust in the air.

Innocence Lost

Love—It is not the fantasy that my youthful heart had dreamed. It is but a pleasurable ghost that touches one's life, only to leave the melancholy of renewed loneliness.

Happiness—It is an elusive state of being that cannot be possessed. She is a temptress who lets us but taste the joy of her, never staying with any one of us.

Time—It is as quick as a dream that one falls into then wakes from, only to find that it is at its end.

Death—It does not carry us to some blissful abode or to eternal suffering. Death is the peace we searched for and hoped to find in life but never did.

Satan's Circle

Oh, such sorrow, oh, such pain,
that can only be relieved by giving it away.

Guilt from the sharing, relief from the same,
compounds the sorrow and intensifies the pain.

Tears for the tears that you know you have
caused, repeat themselves when Satan calls.

The Plague

Dark desire that plagues the mind, hidden by normality, the façade that protects the crime.

Light of redemption fades in the strife when the cloak of obsession falls over our lives.

Compulsion toward might, resistance to slight, morality forsaken for momentary delight.

The Darkness

1. It is insidious. It begins with the romantic fantasy of adolescence being crushed by the reality of commitment's fragility. To love, and with it the hope of being loved, loses its charm.

2. There follows a sense of separation from one's world, in particular from other human beings.

3. An obsessive self-preoccupation develops into a self-imposed isolation, which envelops the victim in a cocoon of solidified self-defense mechanisms.

4. A darkness that obscures the light of redemption falls. A darkness that weighs heavily, taxing the body with a burden that pains every physical movement.

5. Eventually, paralysis of the emotions is complete, leaving only the numbness of indifference. The consciousness is left entombed in a distant place with only one companion—hopelessness.

Resolution

Dark, descending pathways to a dark, cerebral cave

Exits sealed by the collapse of hope

Idealism abandoned

Realism realized

A place where no heroes live, no saviors descend, no love breathes life

No tools of survival, only a flickering will to live—feeble in the face of stagnation's sweet song

A promise of resolution, a tempting sleep, beckons one to exchange his struggle for restful peace.

The Journey

An endless journey in search of peace,
Which always seems just out of reach

A hope for Love that will not die,
Which seems destined to be denied

A search for faith, a fall from grace
Repeat themselves along the way

A ray of hope that shines ahead
Gives us strength to not give in

Perhaps contentment has a price,
Which we must pay by living life

Perhaps this journey is just a task
In payment for a love that lasts.

Achievement's Folly

Old friend Struggle,
Old master of deceit,
Forever dangling freedom just out of reach.

Forcing focused vision,
So the truth cannot be seen:
Our labor is the treasure,
Not the vision that we see.

Second Chance

Life creeps up on us
And opens new doors,
Which lead us to new places,
New struggles, and new rewards.

If fortune shines upon us,
A friendship comes our way,
A stranger who's not a stranger
In some strange, familiar way.

A companion to share our future,
Who understands our pain,
And revels in our joys,
For our pasts are much the same.

A giving heart and loving eyes
That appreciate our charms,
A forgiving presence that understands
And accepts our human flaws.

The Garden

Once along this journey,
I came upon a place
Distant in my soul
Where my wounded heart had hid away.

Alone, a single flower bloomed
In a field of much debris—
So odd, I feared to touch it;
Beauty often does deceive.

Finally, I touched it,
Or somehow it touched me.
With that touch it proliferated;
The flower became a tree.
And from its roots a garden grew,
Which soon encircled me.

Those haunting whispers from the past,
Once my constant foes,
Faded by Love's persistent song
As I let the garden grow.

I pondered how this could be,
I finally felt the breeze…

God's own breath had carried
Across my great stone wall
A single blessed seed.

Endless

I woke one morning to a televised CNN report announcing that the world had come to an end. It was a short broadcast that went into static.

I tried to obtain some additional information on the radio, but apparently, I was too late. On all channels—only static.

I made my morning coffee in the reliable old $10.99 Black & Decker coffee maker. Before I finished my first cup, I noticed, outside my window, that the horizon was a glorious red, which seemed to be covering the morning sky, like a brush fire on a windy day. I finished my coffee and returned to bed, snuggling up against my wife's body.

The heat that woke me was so intense; my skin had erupted into a rash, and I was sweating profusely, as if melting away. I drew closer to my wife, whose presence gave me comfort in the face of unavoidable death. She moved about a few times, perhaps disturbed by the impending doom, but really as she always did in her sleep.

The force of the brilliant light, which vaporized our bodies into simple elements, never woke her. We left that life without much discomfort. I left that life doing the thing I loved most, holding her in my arms.

I woke to a different consciousness, like a dream of sorts. My wife was sitting on a small boulder by a creek. I watched her from a distance as she reached down, letting the water run through her fingers. I explored the surrounding woodlands and found rocks speckled with different colors, which I had to show her. Her eyes sparkled with an excitement as intense as my own. As I walked away, I glanced back to see her smiling.

And so we spent our time until a darkness came. I held her again as this darkness engulfed us. I needed that comfort only she could provide.

Once again, I woke, but in an unfamiliar form. I was now a mountain laurel growing beside a creek. I tried to move but could not. I struggled with my new form and my new limitations. Then I noticed beside me a magnificent mountain laurel, in full bloom, enjoying the fertility of the soil and the blessing of the sun. It was my wife, showing me how to adjust to this new form and providing me with comfort.

A thousand years had passed, but little had changed...

Always

Though you may not know me, I'm sure to be around…

I may speak to you as thunder, as a Red Tail's haunting cry, as the soft sound of a Downy's peck upon a nearby tree, or as the rushing of the water down an endless mountain creek.

Perhaps I'll touch your body as a cool breeze passing by, as the gentle rain of an April shower that catches you by surprise, or as the kiss of a butterfly that lands upon your cheek, then is quickly swept away by the changing of the breeze.

Perhaps I'll be the remains of summer that falls down from the trees, reminding you of the times we danced among the colored leaves.

Possession

I had purchased this property without walking much of it, so I decided that it was time to explore it properly. It was a little cold when I first arrived, but I warmed up once I was off on my expedition. By following the creek, I made it all the way down to the far end of the property. The creek was full of stones of varying sizes, from small pebbles to boulders as large as midsize automobiles. I frequently looked back and was fascinated by how even a few yards changed my perception of the creek and surrounding area, offering new and surprising views of what I had just seen. Near the end of the property, there was a great fork in the creek, which had created an island. It was likely formed by the rushing flood waters during a recent storm. The island can only be reached by jumping across a few boulders.

The mature mountain forest consisted mainly of oaks. These giant guardians of the earth had roots like an endless underground matrix holding the mountains in place, and branches that reached so far into space that they appeared as simple etchings against the winter sky. On my way back, I decided to cut through the middle of the hollow.

Looking down, I realized that I was in a spot where Christmas ferns, in winter wilt, were so thick that it was difficult not to step on them. To avoid causing damage, I went up and traveled along the slope. Going up and down the slope took the wind out of me. After resting for a bit, I continued through the hollow toward the campsite. There were two underground streams constantly seeping up through the ground. I had to cross these areas on the way back or else face the slope. These bogs created a microenvironment of sorts. I noticed that few trees had a chance of survival. Many had fallen due to the moisture in the ground. They lay about in varying stages of decay. I was not sure what grew here in season. It would be interesting to see what plants appreciate this kind of soil. I made my way across by jumping from one fallen tree to the next.

Within a couple hundred feet of the campsite, I noticed some interesting rock outcroppings on the hillside. With my last bit of energy, I struggled up to them. My efforts were rewarded with a view of the campsite, the creek, and part of the hollow. I sat there for the longest time. The isolation and the tranquility of this place were hypnotizing. It had a haunting feeling to it. It made me think about how many creatures (human and otherwise) have passed this way since the beginning of time. It was as if I felt some presence that I couldn't name. It did not evoke fear; instead, it cloaked me with a sense of peace. My mind simply cleared. It was like a perfect state of meditation, something I have read about but have never experienced. It was not a state that I conjured up by chanting or praying. It was as if it sought me out and overwhelmed the chaos in my mind. I felt as if I might dematerialize and transform into something, like a bit of the breeze, a part of the soil, or perhaps one of the many boulders that were scattered about. I almost felt like I wanted this to happen.

I was prevented from dematerializing by a sudden and loud sound. It was deer making their way through the brush. In that quietness, the deer sounded like great monsters walking through the woods, crushing trees under foot. The deer were beautiful but somewhat anticlimactic, considering their thunderous introduction. When a deer looks upon a human being, it seems so fearful, as if it has no clue that it is the more powerful creature. The fear in its eyes seemed familiar...too familiar. I looked away so as not to shame it or so as not to shame myself; I wasn't sure which.

By the time the deer had disturbed me, the sun had gone down behind the mountain. I guess I was lucky they came along; I had not realized that I was freezing. I worked my way down the slope and to the campsite, continuing on to where the Jeep was parked. All the while, it seemed as if something was calling to me, beckoning me back, as if I was not supposed to leave. Perhaps one day the call will be too enticing. Perhaps one day I will become a bit of the breeze, a part of the soil, or perhaps a boulder.

God's Postcard

On my way to Goshen, where the frosty foothills lie, a glitter caught my eye—explosions of reflections across the eastern sky, a kaleidoscope of brilliance that told of some surprise.

I climbed up Nature's stairway, where bitter winter waits. Its vibrant chill called my soul from its resting place.

Up into the Heavens, under cover of the night, an icy gale had raged and left a sparkling crystal realm near Gabriel's open gates.

In the glory of the Morning Star, expelling frozen breath, my eyes beheld the wonder of God's artistic hand in a picture-perfect postcard of an arctic wonderland.

Why He Made Me Wait

I grew weary of running from him, so I stopped to rest and wait, but he sat at a distance as if to contemplate.

I tried to rush toward him, but it became a game of chase.

Then, as if by cue, he stopped and turned to meet me face-to-face.

And in that final moment, I came to understand that Death has a master who has a master plan.

The Final Lullaby

> It's time to go to sleep
> It's time to go to sleep
> It's time to close your eyes
> And time to go to sleep

It's time to rest my weary mind and finally find that peace that evaded me throughout my life like a phantom in a dream.

That phantom, now my escort, that thing that most would fear, is the thing that I had searched for and finally now appears.

That dark, cloaked figure expands his massive, feathered reach, engulfs me in his winged embrace, and there I find eternal peace.

We soar through time unmeasured, then land upon a crest in a world with no worries, no fears, and no regrets.

That whisper from the other side now clearly speaks my name, announcing my arrival to that expanse of endless space.

Here no human form exists, just that spark that once gave life. It merges with a cosmic force of universal light.

Epitaph

Here lies a warrior

Who resided in his temple of solitude

Guarded by his shield of past hurt

His weapons were his lessons well learned

www.ingramcontent.com/pod-product-compliance
Lightning Source LLC
Chambersburg PA
CBHW021134080526
44587CB00012B/1279